Other La Caille Nous Titles

Pick-Up Lines
0-9718191-5-7; July 2003

Backfield in Motion
0-9718191-3-0; Nov. 2002

The Canon of Loose Canons
0-9718191-2-2; Nov. 2002

When He Calls
0-9647635-9-1; July 2002

Father's Footsteps
0-9718191-1-4; July 2002

Bard From Par Taken
0-9718191-0-6; June 2002

Water in a Broken Glass
0-9647635-7-5; Sept. 2000

When You Look At Me
0-9647635-6-7; June 2000

Temples
0-9647635-5-9; Feb. 1999

The Masks of Flipside
0-9647635-4-0; May 1998

The A# Blu's
0-9647635-2-4; Sept. 1996

My Baby's Father
0-9647635-8-3; April 2001 (revd.)

The Eye of the Tornado

*

fifty poems for rhyme and reason

The Eye of the Tornado

fifty poems for rhyme and reason

*

Michelle J. Pinkard

La Caille Nous

Publishing Company

Edited by Guichard Cadet

Cover Design: Keith Saunders for Marion Designs

Library of Congress Cataloging-in-Publication Data

Pinkard, Michelle J., 1977-
  The eye of the tornado : fifty poems for rhyme and reason / Michelle J. Pinkard.
    p. cm.
  ISBN 0-9718191-6-5 (pbk. : alk. paper)
  I. Title.
  PS3616.I57E94 2003
  811'.6--dc21

                                    2003051490

La Caille Nous Publishing Company

Editorial   *Media & Distribution*
PO Box 1004   328 Flatbush Avenue, Suite 240
Riverdale, MD 20738   Brooklyn, NY 11238
www.lcnpub.com   212-726-1293
                                     media@lcnpub.com

Dedication

To God be the praise for the inspiration to write
To Michael, my brother, my twin soul in the fight

To my parents who conceived the dream
To my friends who believed the dream

To my aunts who nurtured it
To my uncles who protected it

And, to all the sweet spirits who
crossed my path while chasing dreams

Upward and onward with love.

The Eye of the Tornado

fifty poems for rhyme and reason

Table of Contents:

The Aftermath
-surveying the damage, rebuilding

The Sunshine
-dancin' under the rainbow

To the Tornado fighters:

Not the ferocity of its tantrum, or the weight of its power.
Not the life threatening winds and rain, the thunder or storm clouds.
Not even the trail of destruction crying the memory of its visit.

These things fail to impress me most about the Tornado, proof of the strength found in Mother Nature.

No, it's the Tornado fighters who climb out from under the rubble to tell the story of their small victory. Though their home was rocked and their faith was tested, they faced the Tornado and lived to tell the tale. They will move on and they will rebuild, proof of the strength found in human nature.

Everyday, we face the Tornado. These forces thrashing all around us. Hate, love, racism, war, joy, pain, success, failure, socialism and freedom, life and death. These powerful forces that we all strive to understand and control. These powerful forces that are beyond understanding, that are beyond control.

Yet, we be the Tornado fighters.

We be the ones who are greeted in the morning by the Tornado, but still find the courage to get out of bed.

We be the ones who trip and fall over the Tornado, but get up and continue on our journey.

We be the ones who make it through the winds and rains, battered and bruised, to the eye of our storm. The Tornado fighters find safety and peace in the midst of it. We cry when the world is laughing. And muster the strength to smile in the wake of our tears.

We be the ones who move on.

Who rebuild.

We be the Tornado fighters.

The Calm

*

the weatherman
predicts showers

Grandpa Jack

Grandpa Jack was a big man.
He would sit at his big oak desk
with a big stack of papers, surrounded
by big certificates in big frames
reading big books filled with
big knowledge. He was a big man.

Sometimes, the grandchildren would
seek small answers to big questions.
Grandpa Jack would lean back in
his big black chair. He would pat
his big belly filled with fried chicken
and penny candy, roll his big eyes back
in his big head to find the knowledge.
And for hours, the children sat and
sighed, in his bigness.

Grandpa Jack used a lot of big words.
He spoke of freedom and education,
of oppression and liberation, of choices
and dedication. Of love. His lessons
from the past were designed
to secure my future. He told me
I had big responsibilities ahead.

Then, one day, Grandpa Jack fought
the big fight with the Big "C." and lost.
His big belly swelled and fell. His big
laugh faded. His big speeches slurred.

His big heart stopped.
His big spirit moved on.

But Grandpa Jack's legacy lives on
as I seek big answers to small questions.
As I write of freedom, education
oppression, liberation, choices and
dedication. As I write of love. I sigh
and remember how big a man
Grandpa Jack really was.

*

The Poets

Beware earthlings, I say thee beware!
there are aliens among you
The Poets are a people from a new planet
                          an old planet
they have come to seduce you
they have come to consume you
Beware earthlings, I say thee beware!

The Poets have big eyes that
see in, out, around and through
they see poetry in sun and moon
in falling leaves and sun sprinkled streams
in joy and pain, in the refrain of
children's laughter. In war chatter
The Poets have big eyes

and ears that shoot up like
antenna and hone in with sonic
frequencies on truth hidden in lies.
on whimpering justice under hypocritical
rubble. on songs seeping from
ocean shores or wind whistles.
The Poets have big ears

and mouths that speak in
different codes to entrance their
prey (Their most cunning of
characteristics, by the way). Their
language a labyrinth of metaphors

and similes, hyperbole and alliteration.
of liberation. The Poets have big mouths.

They have weaknesses, The Poets.
they lie awake at night, dreaming.
their stomachs are screaming and hungry
wanting to be fed, to be fulfilled. their
thoughts are too wide for one head
their hearts are too heavy for one body
they must give of themselves to stay whole.

Beware earthlings, I say thee beware!
The Poets are among you. They want your
young and old. They want your minds and souls
The Poets are a people from a new planet
                              an old planet.
The pen, their gun, they will take control!
Beware earthlings, I say thee beware!

                                        *

21

I've seen God

I've seen God
>   In the mountainous waterfalls of Oregon
>   sitting in small caves orchestrating
>   a singing brook sculpting huge trees
>   and chatting with the wind.

I've seen God
>   Demanding the sleepy sun to rise
>   over the plateaus of Texas while
>   riding black stallions bareback through
>   swallowing flat planes that lead to
>   the end of the earth and back.

I've seen God
>   Walking barefoot where blue water
>   kisses the brown sand beaches of California.
>   And sun rays sprinkle golden pinches
>   of fairy dust onto the ocean that
>   carries life because it is life.

I've seen God
>   In the fields and backyards of Nebraska
>   playing snowman at the dusk of a storm
>   Lifting small chunks of cloud off
>   the ground, holding them high in the air
>   and melting nourishment all over.

I've seen
>   Painting sunsets over Nevada

with splashes of purple, red, orange
and blue. Using long, detailed,
wide strokes while sitting atop a rock
surrounded by nothing but
space, time, and cacti.

I've seen God
Playing peek-a-boo with alligators
in the swamps of Louisiana and
holding night conferences with
crickets while baking crawfish
mud pies in the ground.

When I see God
I wave one sometimes two hands
in the air just to say hello because
Momma always said it was rude
not to speak. So, I wave, and say
'Good day God, See you tomorrow.'

A Letter to a College Friend

I sometimes sit and reminisce about you
and our time together.

Many memories to choose from all
rooted in our own quest of knowledge.

Thought we had the world figured,
boxed. thought we were going to set
things right.

Years later, I find that I keep passing
the starting point of our circle.

What I learned yesterday, takes
new form today. And is something
completely different
tomorrow

When did the answers stop being
black and white? Who knew there were
so many shades of gray?

I hope your dreams realized. Mine? They
seem to change with political season.

Kiss the children
and warn them for me.

That courage works best when fear is near
Change is a steady companion, but tradition
is a worthy guide.

*

For Toot

I admired your beauty, awed that
you never knew the power of it.
I envied it. marveled in it,
was drawn to it. Studied it.
Was crushed when they stole it.
I watched you sit in class, too
Listening to White teachers tell you
fairy tales and happy endings.
Never understanding
In your world, you know not
a frog that turns into a prince
But of a 14 year old boy
Telling you to suck his 14 year old dick
And for the love you never found
you let him explore native jungles
and premature fruits
Not for the sake of probing fingers
But for creation
New life to blur vision of old world
       Yes, I watched, I wondered
          I cried.

*

The truth about cliché's

The truth about cliché's
is that there is little truth in them
And, though, by day
they are designed to comfort
At night they only seem to destroy

It's all for the best
is usually said when you are at your worst
You made your bed
ignores the lies told to you in it
Follow your heart
means little without head copiloting
This too shall pass
mentions nothing of the meantime
Distance makes the heart grow fonder
is a mere ploy when love goes weaker

But I must find real strength
in the superficial cliché 'cuz
Leaving you and our bed
was for the best.
And, I must follow my heart
until the pain passes
from of our time
and distance apart.

Money's worth

When I was young
as babes oft do
I'd ask my parents
'bout jobs they'd cling to.

Dad packed cow shit
ignored the bowel hell
when his kids ran away
said it was money's smell.

Mom cooked large meals
and bled in hot kitchens
She'd say t'was money
that caused her afflictions.

If money smells of shit
and feels of scabs girth
then tell this young babe
how much is it worth?

*

I wanna taste me some freedom

I wanna taste me some freedom
want it to melt on the tip of my tongue
and fizz like orange soda pop
on sunny summer afternoons.

Gettin' sick of swallowing processed lies
force-fed moldy afterthoughts on stale bread
Just give me a sample of some of that freedom
and nourish me a little on my long journey

Mmmmm, I wanna taste me some freedom.

Is it cold and creamy, that freedom
like chocolate chip cookie dough ice cream
or sugary sweet
like bubble gum cotton candy?

Is it hot hot hot
like jalepeno peppers
or intoxicating
like Jack Daniel's whiskey?

Oh! I need to taste me some freedom.

Does freedom melt in your mouth
like candy coated M & Ms
or stick to the roof
like Jiffy peanut butter sandwiches?

Yeah, I'm gonna taste me some freedom
gonna take me a big o' chunky bite
gonna let it fill me all the way up
Til' I just can't take no more.

*

Soul Food

I don't care what dem health fools say
Fried food is da only way
Puts a smile on yo' face
Gives yo' tummy a warm embrace
It's a good end to a bad day.

Save your talk of heart disease
Can't ya' see I'm tryin' to be happy?
So pass me some of dem collard greens
And a heapin' helpin' of dem black-eyed-peas
And some butta' milk biscuits, if ya please.

Away with talk of size and scales
I'm a victim of all dem smells
Sweet surrender to candied yams
Spicy chitlins,' chicken and dumplins'
I plead guilty to my culinary sin.

*

Getting there

It may take a week
but I'll get there
to that quiet place
where time is lost
and space don't cost
one cent of sanity.

It may take a month
but I'll find it
that special key
unlocks life's mysteries
and simple pleasures
aren't temporary
like the breeze.

It may take a year
but I'll see it
the sea of serenity
where calm floats on lily pads
and dreams don't go bad
where truth swims upstream
justice sings a sweet lullaby
young freedom plays on cherry tree branches.

It may take a lifetime
but one day, it will be all mine
joy beyond bounds
where love showers down
in candy-coated rain drops

and streets are lined with gold.
it's where wings sprout liberation
movement is worth celebration
and happiness isn't bought or sold.

*

The Beginning

*

it feels like rain

Small talk

don't give me no small talk; laced with subtlety and weak smiles
don't want to know your worldly name; or what part of the earth you claim
don't want to make conversation; I need it to grow from truth
don't give me no small talk; I need a voice that isn't limping and lame.

I want talk that's so big that even Washington can't claim it
so wide human nature must face it; talk so tall, it shames the mountains
I want talk that grows from rain puddles, to ponds, to lakes
talk that flows like streams, to rivers, to oceans

I want talk that's so big

no whisper, no murmur, no soft lull in the black of night will do
Give me screams, Give me thunder, Give me a beacon brighter than the sun
words that stir and simmer and bubble, like water to the teapot
before the steam, before the whistle, before its tears overrun

I want talk that's so big
talk that's so big
talk that's so powerful
that's so powerful
powerful
I want talk that's so free
free and liberating
liberating
and big

I want talk that's everything, and anything
but small.

*

Staying informed

Turned on the television today
So I can stay informed.
I should know what's going on
I should know what lies in store.

But what I was pressed to discover
was more senseless than ignorance.
The knowledge I so eagerly sought
was fraught with lies and pretense.

When did the peace of religion
Become reason for murder and war?
When did young babes become enemy
and innocence the prey at death's door?

No. I think it best to turn the tele off
and keep my pen and pad in hand.
And, hopefully, revolution can begin
with one mind, one voice, and one pen.

*

The things you said

I heard old love songs
play over and over again
in my head.

All morning thoughts
were of you and of all
the things you said.

You talked of gentle kisses
salt sweaty hands
atop a satin laced bed.

Your words stirred in me
waking my romantic core
from the dead.

And just when I thought
lust was the only motive
by which you were led.

You said my love
was your greatest fantasy
and one day we would wed.

*

One Thursday night in April

One Thursday night in April
you approached me sugary sweet
your mouth uttered words tender
your courage danced with my soul meek.

One Thursday night in April
I released my caged spirit
I blossomed a perfumed rose
My smile and your touch fit.

One Thursday night in April
A kiss unleashed the spell
A hand the wand for magic
A moan dictated the tale.

One Thursday night in April
A time to set free virginity
I gave you my secret treasures
you gave me peace and serenity.

*

Computer Screen

Can you see me
behind my smoky computer
screen of smoke
my smoke screen

Can you see my luscious lips
my curvaceous size six hips
stand at attention tits
and sizzling ready clit
In that smoky computer screen
that computer screen of smoke
that smoke screen

Can you see my dancing chest
that I really do fuck the best
how well I can drive my stick
and shift to make you tick
In that smoky computer screen
that computer screen of smoke
that smoke screen

Or do you see me
Body, mind and soul Three-D
Whose pudgy but sweet
fragile but discrete
hiding behind a smoky computer screen
a computer screen of smoke
a smoke screen.

*

When I am at work…

When I am at work… and sitting still in my
rightly angled cubicle…which gives me just
enough privacy for illusion and…reveals just
enough to satisfy Boss that I am still sitting still
…and I stare at that computer for a really long
time….just enough time…it begins to happen…

…the paragraphs become sentences…the
sentences become fragments….the fragments
become words….. the words, letters….the letters
dance independently around the screen and began
to swirl…like a whirlpool….no…tornado…NO!
a volcano…..yes, yes… a volcano!…

…turning red and swirling red…and bubbling
and swirling and swirling and swirling and
bubbling red …until…they pour out of the screen
and onto my 'oh-so-neat-for-the-Boss desk…
charring the blue and black pens and paper clips
    ….onto my lap…

…burning my crotch….reminding me it's been a while
since my crotch has burned for anything or anyone….
up to my heart, (it too yearns to burn)…and into my head,
my head….it burns so hot it scorches my whole rightly
angled cubicle…it burns so red and burns so much…
that even though…all I am doing is sitting still….
I realize I probably should have called in sick today.

Workin' in the shadows of freedom

Stuck at work
riding the clock
tick tock tick tock
The master's strings
aren't that tight today
giving my mind
room to play
and remember
freedom.

Those sweet days
when the time
was all mine
when rainbows rested
on gummy bears
and lemon heads
and finding peace
was easy 'cuz
there was no shortage
of freedom.

Those days are gone
like some cool
jazzy summer song
whispers in the wind
seconds gone
places been
nothing's left but daily grind
hopes of security

* the eye of the tornado *

replace memories
of freedom.

*

Penis envy

I was standing alone on
the corner waiting for the
light to tell me to go, all by
myself alone. Thinking of
me and just enjoying being
a woman all by my woman
self. With one hand on my
hip the other checking
the time. My mind was on
my fineness, my lips, my eyes
the line of my thighs, fine.
Then I felt you enjoying me
being a woman too. I mean,
look at you peeping and
beeping as I cross the street.
disrespecting Me.

    I

         was

               almost

                      DISTRACTED

              from

       being

  a

woman enjoying her woman
self. Then I remembered
my fineness. How the sway
of my attaché compliments
my sashay. And how good
it feels to be a woman all

by my woman self. As I
cross the street I smile. All
the while knowing and owning
just how much that Penis
in the car envies me.

*

A Scream Unheard

I have a song
so beautiful, so distinct
so powerful, that even the
nightingale would close its beak
and be comforted by
green silence.
But, it drowns
in the clacking, shacking,
building, destroying,
business of a millennium world.

My words are
sharper than any sword
the message inspired
by a staff strong enough
to part seas.
Alas, I can't afford
to put it on billboards
or in electrical boxes

So, I strengthen myself
to move mountains
conjure smiles
enlighten darkness and
breathe life into death.
But that too must wait.
Right now I am too busy
surviving.

*

A dream challenged and failed

Curious about the dream deferred?
Well, what about a dream challenged and failed?
Where does all the hope go
when the ship lifted anchor and sailed?
Is there some lost island
        where dreams swing free on tropical vines?
Maybe they sit in some taboo prison
        and sing chain gang songs of love divine.
Perhaps they find some peace
        beneath unmarked graves in dark cemeteries.

The dream deferred is sad, tis true,
yet somehow keeps the goal
The dream that's challenged and failed
can do nothing but explode.

                                                *

The Wrath

*

on finding shelter and
fighting back

So glad slavery is over
(a poem meant to offend)

I'm so glad slavery is over
cuz' we don't have to answer
to the Massah' and the Misses'
anymore. So glad we don't
have to check our pride at the
door to feed our families
and cloak our backs anymore.
So glad that system came
crashing down like a house
of mirrors causing 400 years
of bad luck. Yeah.
I'm so glad slavery is over.

> *No more auction block for me,*
> *No more, no more,*
> *No more auction block for me,*
> *Many thousand gone.*

I'm so glad slavery is over
though it took 'em a couple
of years to tell us what we
already knew. We free. We free.
But they couldn't let us be
Said' we still owe. Built their
country with bloody hands, but
we still owe. We still owe?
Just can't be bought

and sold no mo.' Yeah,
I'm so glad slavery is over.

> *No more peck of corn for me,*
> *No more, no more,*
> *No more peck of corn for me,*
> *Many thousand gone.*

I'm so glad slavery is over
cuz' they can't beat us anymore.
Well, not on camera anyway.
And they can't lynch and murder us
like they did a few years ago in Jasper
South. And they can't plot to
burn our institutions using counterfeit
money and counterfeit ideals. Yeah,
I'm so glad slavery is over.

> *No more pint of salt for me,*
> *No more, no more,*
> *No more pint of salt for me,*
> *Many thousand gone.*

I'm so glad slavery is over
cuz' they knew we had the spirit
of Africa, Africa. Africa!
beating inside us. The sovereignty
of the Lion over his territory
The patience of his lioness
biding her time, biding her time
before she pounces. Yeah,

I bet they so glad slavery
is over, too.

No more driver's lash for me,
No more, no more,
No more driver's lash for me,
Many thousand gone.

Hmmph, yes, things are better, now
that slavery is over. We have a
new system. I work from dawn til' dusk
he gives me a weakly allowance
that I give back, to feed my family,
and cloak my back. All the while
I gotta show my teeth, to keep the peace.
But at least, I am not bought and sold
no mo.' Yeah, not bought and sold.
I'se sooo glad slav'ry is ovuh!

*

***Note: The stanza's in italics are taken from a slave song called, "No more auction block for me." The author is unknown. It has been reprinted in countless anthologies and works.*

RE: Casual Friday

Please? no more jeans
on casual Friday. WE
have decided that
individuality -
even for one day -
is not Okay.

Please. wear robotic
grays and blues
nothing new to
pursue mind-numbing
duplicity.

Pleeasee! I don't feel
gray or blue
I am red. I am green.
yellow. I am Black.
and that, today and always
is Okay.

*

Disconnected

Saw a man today
outside the corner store
He was pissed at some oppressor
Or maybe at all of them.

His tantrum was thick
He was disconnected
      disillusioned
          dissatisfied
Yes, he was dissed.

I am sure others thought him victim
Chained to psychosis and paranoia.

I thought him free
Free from collectors
Free from the daily mundane
Free from fear
And free to talk about his damnation.

But, I had no time to listen
Rent payment is over due
had groceries to buy
a phone bill to pay
before, I too, became disconnected.

                                           *

Freedom

My brother stepped to me
with a gun in one hand
empty bag in the other
Said, Gimme your Freedom Sister,
Cuz I done lost mine

But where did you keep it, I said.
Perched on the front porch
Unguarded for any demon to steal.

Or was your Freedom dangling
around your neck
honey-dipped in gold
binding like a yoke to a bull

Did you place your Freedom
in rolling paper
swallow it in one big gulp
and let it evaporate in smoke

Retrace your steps, my brother
I am sure your Freedom waits
shivering in some dark corner
or swimming upstream
in a river of red wine

As for me, death first
Before I give away any
of my Freedom.

A Poem for Allissa Brown

I never saw the sun
        shine on your little brown face
Never heard you laugh
        at dancin' dinosaurs
                or sing ABC songs

Until the news broke today
        dear child
        Never even knew your name.

They say you were riding along one night
        probably sleeping, dreaming of
        fairies and fireflies.
When a man named Sudds
        whose history was anything but clean
                spit a storm of bullets into your sun shined life

There are no more dreams
        no more fairies, dinosaurs or fireflies
The sun will never shine for you
The world will never know your spirit
        but your innocence will surely be missed

So, when the 6 o'clock news signs off
        And the papers worn weary of footnotes
Here is to your sweet life, dear child
        However short your visit may have been.

*

Dandelions

I dreamed of dandelions
not predictable roses
or purple tulips
but bright yellow dandelions
perched in patches of green grass.

The flower of my youth
those bright yellow dandelions
would grow faster than I could pick 'em
to make bouquets for Momma
or headdresses for my doll Delilah.

Then, one day
he poured poison on my dandelion
told me they was nothin'
but unwanted weeds
And made me watch
her as she withered
died and left me.

But I will remember the dandelion
with all the youthful glory I gave her
She was beauty bountiful
wrapped in soft yellow clouds
free and innocent
at no cost or pretense
She was all
I dared to dream.

*

Braids

You want to understand my braids
want to know their power
the patience of sitting for hours
until thick hair takes new form.

Walk with me through history's span
See little black boys and girls sit
under their Mamma's hand as she
twists hair, patience and love into new form.

Listen to the crackle of parting hair
meet the beat of the African drum
dance with the beads and shells
as they swing and sway in their new form.

Still don't understand my braids?
or the power and patience of their creation.
In each fold a story of a people who
loves, endures, waits, and struggles for new form.

*

Dirty Draws

You left your dirty draws
the last time we made imitation
watered down love and
I began to look for the signs or
the hidden messages that
you were too afraid or too busy
to say. Were they your returning card,
your reason to stop by. No, you
don't need a reason, besides
my door has always been too open or
Perhaps they were your security deposit
a way to secure a place to hang
both your hat and your draws
Then, maybe, too, it was your way of
marking your territory, but then again
only dogs mark their territory
and I don't recall becoming a territory
for the marking. Or did I.
Maybe, it was just your way of saying
that dirty draws would be all
I can ever have of you.

*

Your kind of Love

Your kind of love
teases like a bright orange carrot
That mocks the caged rabbit.

Your kind of love
tastes like a fireball candy drop
Sweet, at first
but burns all the way down, through and out.

Your kind of love
looks like a cute little pup
That shits all over waxed hardwood floors.

Your kind of love,
     Your kind of love,
          Your kind of love

I can do without.

*

Notes for my Eulogy

If it were said I loved life
          that I could not deny
If it were said I liked life
          that would be a lie.

If it were said I loved to love
          that much would be true
If it were said I trusted love
          then you didn't have a clue.

If it were said I revered the simple things
          that I would adore
If it were said I lived to protect them
          I should have died doing more.

If it were said I was a peace seeker
          that much I hope I found
If it were said I lived life in war
          then pray I'm heaven bound.

Please,
let it be said I took a knife to the stone of life
          like a prisoner without fear
And in its fine granite, I dared to write, yes
          "I was here."

*

The Aftermath

*

surveying the damage,
rebuilding

You know me

You look me lost
confused and dazed
crazed and amazed
at the sight of me
they tried to divide with
selfish lies. Tried to make
you forget, but you
remember me.
You know me.

We drank from the bank
of Lake Tanganyika.
I was your Eve and
together we gave birth
to rhythm, soul, dance
culture and beauty.
We sung of nature
and life and love.
You know me.

I held your hand
in the belly of slave
ships. In your eyes
I saw strength. In mine
you saw hope.
With hope and strength
we would conquer
a new world.
You know me.

Our voices rose
from the dry earth of
cotton fields and reached
the heavens. And when
they lay the whip on
your back, it was me
you thought of. And when
they forced my legs wide,
it was your name I called.
You know me.

I took the Billy club
beside you. I braved the
water hose with you.
The heels of my feet
burned as I marched next
to you. My bloody
fist lifted to the sky
with yours.
You know me.

I share your frustration
I too want to scream
want to holler 'til all
the hurt vomits out of my
stomach onto marble floors.
Can't. Gasping for air
under this sealed tight
razor sharp glass ceiling

All the while seeing
where you want to go
Can't get there
Can't get there.

You know me
     I am that face in the mirror
You know me
     the completion to make life clearer
You know me
You know me
You....me.

*

A poem for Nikki in Giovanni style

You simply rejected rejection
said hell no to oppression
in the sweet spirit of revolution
I dig that.

You were the scream
when they tried to muzzle us
You were the fist
when they tried to handcuff us
You were the truth
when they lied to us
You pushed for revolution
when we were forgetful
That's worth digging into.

Thank you for Nikki-Rosa
Indeed, Black Love is Black Wealth
There's no price tag for Mama's
sweet yams and turnip greens or
Daddy tucking babies into bed
while singing Stevie Wonder songs
And, thank you, for shining our
Beautiful Black Men, who traded in
they afros for new cornrows but still walk
down the street with the same
ol' danger, bringing new pleasures
Yeah, gotta dig that.

Mostly, thank you for your spirit.

You are mother, daughter, sister,
teacher, confidant, dreamer.
You are poetry.
I dig that, too.

*

Reclaiming Diva

The abuse of the word Diva saddens me
obviously done by literary tyrants
who refuse to bow down to the power
of the word. Shame on you.
Diva,
It was a special word
before they captured it
stomped on it
watered it down with adjectives, prefixes
suffixes and pretenses
Diva,
a word so divine
shouldn't be branded on
teeny bopper pop singers
or one-hit wonder 70's queens
no, Diva
should have been reserved
for the goddess whose inner beauty
creates outer beauty
whose class is flawless
and smile is unconditional
whose dress is appealing
but never too revealing
Diva. Ah me!
The abuse of the word
saddens me.

*

Do we love us anymore?

I heard you
sing those same tired blues
"You bitch too much
not supportive enough"
then run to white women to soothe you.

Revelation is knockin at the door
Do we love us anymore

And a word to my sista
who lays with any rich mista
naked in some caddy
turnin tricks with puff daddy
somethin evil's a' brewin' in this new-aged twista.

Revelation is knockin at the door
Do we love us anymore

For my beautiful black children
drowning in a world of sin
cursing before they talk
grown before they walk
has purity and innocence come to an end?

Revelation is knockin at the door
Do we love us anymore

I remember days of old
King and Malcom talked us bold

when black was beautiful
and unity was plentiful
now with blank checks we are bought and sold.

Revelation is knockin at the door
Do we love us anymore

We are lost in a sea of self hatred
ignoring everything the Master said
our mothers are crying
our fathers dying
Wake up, the enemy is in our bed!

Revelation is knockin at the door
Do we love us anymore?

*

One day wiser at the pond

One day wiser at the pond
I took my notebook to write
down its advice. With the tide
came swimming by
three ducks to my feet
                come staring at me

We made our introductions
and obeyed greeting traditions
they shared the story of their lives
but, already knew that of mine

They heard it in the roar of war
planes and the ringing of telephones
insane, in the clicking of clocks
and door locks. Seen it in old
cigarette butts, and in the color
                of sun-lit oil.

We played and laughed our day
away. I peeked to their boo and
we knew that time belonged to
us. And, that was enough, the
 pond, the sun, the ducks
                and me.

Then a fisherman came along
and scoffed at our little song
Looked us crazy, baited his hook

cast his rod and sent ripples
throughout our whole pond.

With a nod, our game was done.
The duck trio swam away, with
their diamond shaved trail shining
the memory. And I took my
notebook and walked the other way.

The fisherman hocked a loogie
picked his nose, reached for his
cell phone, and
            was none the wiser.

                                    *

The Business of Me

I gotta' get back
to the business of me
to watching my withdrawals
securing my deposits

I have to take into account
all of my bad investments
like supplying you with my time
or, not writing off your lies

I must have miscalculated
I thought one-plus-one was two
But you sought extra stock
and now I am seeing red

So. I gotta' get back
to the business of me
to cutting all my losses and
making room for new gains.

*

Fully figured

Club night and feelin' fine
I was out to floss and shine
Wearing my fully figured leopard print skirt
My fully figured come get me black shirt
Stepped out of my fully figured car
To have a good time in that fully figured bar
mmmmmmmmmmm mm mm I was so full
            of intelligence and complexities,
            of style and beautiful vulgarities, I was so full
figured my fullness was enough to stop traffic
figured my fullness should give classes
figured my fullness could stop your hate
figured my fullness was somethin' you can't shake
    yes, it's somethin' you can't shake
            that fully figured side of me
fullness put a bounce in my step
fullness is my crafty little web
fullness put a smile on my lips
fullness put the swish in my hips
mmmmmmmmmmmm mm mm I was so full
            that I couldn't even hear your empty thoughts
I guess you think my head should hang low
You're pissed because confidence is not my foe
I guess you think beauty is factory-produced
You can't fully figure the real and diverse truth
            That's OK, cuz' I got somethin' you can't shake, see
            It's that fully figured, side of me.
As I sit at the end of this fully-figured bar
the stool, my throne, and you

    pleading to enter my Queendom
I can't help but smile.
My grace, my love, my curves, my style.
You couldn't help but stare.
I declare, it's the fully-figured side of me.

                                                              *

A Lady's Mack

Say boy,
Can I peep you?
Can I dig you?
Move that move
lookin' smooth
and shake dat ass
to this funky grove

Hey boy,
Ain't you got no cares?
Ain't you got no fears?
Feel that base
touch my waist
and twirl me 'round
in this hip-hop place.

Wait boy,
Could this be love
In this hypnotic, high-chronic club?
Burnin' desire
feel my fire
and dance that dance
'til our hips get tired.

Say boy,
Can I peep you?
Can I dig you?
Love that smell
got me spelled

and where we go
only this beat can tell.

*

I want a man

I want a man
who says what he means
and means what he says
who knows that truth
shouldn't hide behind sweet lies
that wither in the morning sun.

I want a man
who does what he says
and says what he does
who knows that commitment
isn't a matter of convenience
but a measure of character.

I want a man
who dares to dream
and dreams to dare
who knows success
is a treasure sought
not brought with Tuesday's mail.

I want a man
who loves to live
and lives to love
who knows a woman's heart
should be adorned on living room mantels
not bedroom headboards.

*

You (a failed attempt at a love poem)

You
are a poet's nightmare
a writer's Kryptonite
an author's greatest fear
the pen trembles at
the mere challenge of you.

You
are more than a metaphor
more than calm sunsets
over rolling hills. more than
a chorus of sprinkling streams
and forest birds singing.

You
are more than a noun
you're the place I want to be
your name claims me.
So much so, I must confess
I want it for my own.

You
are more than a verb
your walk shakes me up
and settles me down.
one smile from you turns
gray skies, blue.

*   the eye of the tornado   *

You
it's too bad, too. Because I
really needed to write a love
poem. Perhaps, it's best just to
leave the page pure, clean, and
fresh to capture the essence of
You.

*

The Sunshine

*

dancin' under the rainbow

A poem of reconciliation for Daddy

I heard your song in the distance
I felt its lyrics of yore
I saw your failed attempts
I tasted the pain you bore

Your voice unfamiliar
Your laughter undefended
Your name unidentified
Your presence uncommitted

What are we to do now
Where do we go from here
Why do our souls now tremble
When do we release the fear

Give me your beaten hand
In it I place my beaten heart
By blood, love bound us together
When pride tried to rip us apart.

*

To a special black woman

I saw you for the first time this morning
though I have known you all my life
        and before
I saw you for the first time, just
                this morning
        and knew that it was time for a poem.

I suppose there were snapshots before
like the times you served me
Margaret Walker and peanut butter sandwiches
        with the crust, or
when you taught me how to make
Maya Angelou jambalaya and
                Sojourner Truth bread
said, 'there's a special flava in sistahood that
you just can't taste in Wonder bread.'

Yes, there were glimpses
   of you in smile by candle light
        when lights were cut off and only
our love and a gas stove kept us warm
                through the night.

If there were tears, you never showed them
If there were fears, you never owned them
        you kept your chin up
        when world, (and some of your brothas)
        put you down
said t'was better to live brave, than with a frown

Tried, that I might, put my feet
in your muddy footprint…As you
walked the streets in your own sweet
beat. With your new, true, can do attitude
pulling strength from the shadows of the dark
past. I didn't see, I couldn't see, your effect on me.

And. I heard you. keepin you children and
man
in
line
while singin, playin, workin, prayin, all by yourself
And I heard them call you ugly, then try to steal
your lips, hips, tits and voice.
        I listened and learned.

Yet, it wasn't 'til early this morning, I saw
you, just you, for the first time. after I washed
my face and brushed my hair back. It was
there, in the mirror, that truth reflected me
you looking back at me. Paralyzed. I stood
Aware. Being a black woman is both captivating

        and liberating.
I knew it was time for a poem.

*

His Plan

It wasn't all that long ago
Life hit me with a vicious blow
bad hair, no food,
old shoes, sad mood.
Times are hard with no dough.

Why me was the blanket of my cry
dismayed, there was no reply
go beg, go steal,
go cheat, go kill,
Pain inhaled in every sigh.

And how mighty they would laugh
As sure as I would pass
broke girl, hood rat,
dirt poor, door mat,
Praying nightly this would not last.

Then He came and held my hand
Said by my side He would always stand
The Ghost, the Love,
The Book, The Blood,
Feels good to be included in His plan.

*

Diggin' on me

I like me
from the nap of my hair
to the sole of my feet
the span of my hands
the curl of my lips sweet
Yes, I do have flare
I like me

I like me
from the bounce of my breast
to the ride of my ass
mmm mmm mmm
I am so so bad
Yes, I must confess
I like me

I like me
from the dance of my hips
to the intensity of my eyes
the richness of my skin
the tease of my thighs
Yes, I do have gifts
I like me

*

Forgotten Memories

I can barely recall
the tease of your touch
or how easily I would blush
at your smile.

I hardly remember
that delicious sexy tone
or how softly you moaned
my name.

I have already forgotten
the sweet taste of your lips
and the swirl of your hips
against mine.

I believe it faded away
the hold of your love
like a rain cloud above
fleeing sunrise.

And, I am made whole
as your half disappears
save the room it rears
for new love.

*

The Club

Crowded room
smoky air
jazzy, sexy
atmosphere.
Hear that singer
go scat scat scat
hear those drums
go did-dat tat tat.
Feel my hips shake
and my shoulders
gyrate.
Gonna' have a funky
good time in this
be-bop, hip-hop
club tonight.

Madam bartender
vodka with a twist
just a little ice
stirred not shaken
and a splash of
somethin' nice.
If you please.
Gonna' have a funky
good time in this
be-bop, hip-hop
club tonight.

Bathroom check
watch the dress
gloss the lips
check the tits
tease the hair
oh, my
I do have flare.
Gonna' have a funky
good time in this
be-bop, hip-hop
club tonight.

It's him
my new fan
my future man
that stranger across
the room.
With the lock of our eyes
he peeks at the secrets
of my soul.
            Come to me
            Come to me
A touch of the hand
our mating dance begins.
Gonna' have a funky
good time in this
be-bop, hip-hop
club tonight.

                                    *

Love Making

I love our conversations
after we make love
when you take my hand
in your hand and
guide me though the labyrinth
of your love, your life
and your past lives.

I love tracing the
curve of your smile
as you trace the curve
of mine. And how it makes
me shine an ocean deep
and a treasure's keep of innocence,
wisdom and peace.

I love the rhythm of your laugh
how it makes your eyes open wide
to show flashes of your soul
and how it vibrates through our
christened bed, sheets and pillows
to tickle up my very own laugh.

I love watching your hands
dance with causality and clarity
as we rate the latest song,
latest music, latest movie.
Or, trip on southern livin', or a lazy
boss, or how some folks floss which

leads to the stalled career of
Bobby Brown.
         Bobby Brown?

I love smelling the intensity
of your tone, like the moan
you gave me minutes ago,
when we fall serious and
talk about the future of Our People and
how Black Fate, Black Love,
Black Life has become
Black Listed.

I love our conversations
after we make love
because it is then that
our love making
begins.

                                                    *

A little rain for my soul

Sometimes
>   I don't bother hiding my head in the rain
>   I let the tears fall down from heaven
>   and wash my face clean.

I figure
>   if rain nurtures the flowers
>   if showers help green grass to grow
>   surely it must be good for my soul.

Cold breezes
>   won't slow the dance in my beat
>   won't slur the rhythm of my feet
>   or make me stumble in defeat.

I know
>   where I've been, where I want to be
>   I got to keep going, keep moving
>   if I am to succeed.

Gray clouds
>   can't stop me from shining
>   can't keep me from singing with India or Jill
>   or make me doubt His will.

Sometimes
>   even the sun needs a break
>   just a little time to rejuvenate
>   to beam brighter than before.

Our song

I love our style
  Doin' it well, with a cool, jazzy smile
    Pimp Strut,
            Smooth cuts,
Stare at me for a little while.

I love our beat
  Everything we do with our feet
    Jackson's walk,
            Gregory's tap,
The rhythm makes my soul complete.

I love our laugh
  Overshadowing the pain we mask
  Cosby's subtlety,
            Pryor's vulgarity,
Bold contagious, our presence will never pass.

I love our memory
  A history too strong for mystery
    Tubman, Scott
            Turner, King
Many walked before us to pass the key.

I love our hands
  Conquered cotton's span
    Coarse touch,
            Loving much,
A hold as strong as the mother land.

I love our name
  Beautifully Black--Should I feel shame?
   Proud Afro-,
       Courageous Negro,
By our tradition, our future we claim.

*

For those who still wonder

For those who still wonder
        with dreamy eyes
        and sugar cane smiles

For those who still ache
        for peace of mind
        and piece of heart

For those who still believe
        in good times ahead
        and goodness in man

For those who still care
        about the earth and stars
        the plants and animals

For those who still trust
        that love conquers all
        and pain is only temporary

For those who still dream
        who still seek
        who still pray

You are the best of our yesterday
        the hope for our tomorrow
        and our strength today

                                            *

Epilogue

Dear Mama,

I am strong now. I am better. Of course it was you who taught me I had to be strong, I had to be better, if I were to be at all. Still, in the end. I think it was all those tornadoes we fought together.

Yes, growing up in Omaha, there was a lot of talk of tornadoes. In grade school, they taught us to crawl under our desks, get into the fetal position, and pray the tornado didn't see us. The news anchorwoman taught us to seek shelter and hope the tornado didn't find us. The radio voice taught us to huddle in our basements and hope that tornado didn't land on our house and sweep it away.

But it was you who taught me to face my tornadoes. Nature can't be stopped, you warned. It can't be predicted or controlled. When the winds are fighting around you, when life is throwing its temper tantrum and safety is hard to find, seek peace in the eye of the storm, you said. Find comfort and courage in its center because there is where you'll find the answer. There is where you'll see things clearly.

And, for that, I am strong. I am better. Thank you.

Peace, Love and Blessings,
Michelle
Michelle J Pinkard
Tornado fighter

About the Author

Michelle J. Pinkard was born in Omaha, Neb., and is an honors graduate of Paul Quinn College in Dallas, Texas where she studied Mass Communication and English. She will pursue her masters degree in Creative Writing at Morgan State University in Baltimore, MD, this fall after being offered a full-scholarship and fellowship. Michelle is currently working on a second volume of poetry and memoir project.

Many of her poems were printed in literary publications across the country, including: Elements Magazine, Poetry Motel, Ya'Sou! A Celebration of Life, Love's Chance Magazine and Struggle Magazine. She is best known for her award-winning work as a print journalist and columnist at The Times of Shreveport in Louisiana.

To learn more about Michelle and upcoming speaking events, visit www.michellejpinkard.com.